Born in Kent in 1929, U. A. Fanthorpe was educated in Surrey and at Oxford. She was Head of English at Cheltenham Ladies' College, and then 'became a middle-aged drop-out in order to write'. Poetry took her by surprise when she started as a clerk/receptionist at a neuropsychiatric hospital in Bristol. Her first collection, *Side Effects*, was published in 1978. From 1983 to 1985 she was the Arts Council Literary Fellow at Lancaster, and in 1994 she was the first woman to be nominated for the post of Professor of Poetry at Oxford. Her seven collections of poetry are all published by Peterloo Poets, and her *Selected Poems* was published as a King Penguin in 1986. Peterloo will be publishing her *Collected Poems* in 2003. U. A. Fanthorpe was awarded the C.B.E. in 2001 for her services to literature.

As a freelance writer since 1987, Fanthorpe gives readings around the country, accompanied by R. V. Bailey, who is the other voice in the Penguin audiotape *Double Act*, and in the British Council/Bloodaxe tape *Poetry Quartets 5*.

*

Nick Wadley trained as a painter and art historian and taught for many years at Chelsea School of Art. His books include *Noa Noa: Gauguin's Tahiti* (1985) and *Impressionist and Post-Impressionist Drawing* (1991). He has worked on exhibitions in London, Europe and Japan, and he now reviews for the *TLS* and other journals. His drawings and cartoons regularly appear in magazines and newspapers.

For Jessica

LULLABY: SANCTUS DEUS

Words by U.A.Fanthorpe
Music by Nigel Dodd

U. A. Fanthorpe

Christmas Poems

with drawings by

Nick Wadley

ENITHARMON PRESS

PETERLOO POETS

2002

First published in 2002
by the Enitharmon Press
26B Caversham Road
London NW5 2DU

www.enitharmon.co.uk

&
Peterloo Poets
The Old Chapel
Sand Lane
Calstock
Cornwall PL18 9QX

Enitharmon edition reprinted 2002

Distributed in the USA and Canada
by Dufour Editions Inc.
PO Box 7, Chester Springs
PA 19425, USA

ISBN 1 900564 13 0 (Enitharmon)
ISBN 1 871471 06 0 (Peterloo)

British Library Cataloguing-in-Publication Data.
A catalogue record for this book is available
from the British Library.

The publishers gratefully acknowledge financial assistance from the
Arts Council of England (Enitharmon) and South West Arts (Peterloo).

Typeset in Poliphilus by Servis Filmsetting Ltd, Manchester
and printed in Great Britain by
Biddles Ltd, *www.biddles.co.uk*

CONTENTS

ACKNOWLEDGEMENTS

Some of these poems appeared in *Poems for Christmas* (1981), *Standing To* (1982), *A Watching Brief* (1987), *Safe as Houses* (1995) and *Consequences* (2000), all published by Peterloo Poets.

INTRODUCTION

The advantage of Christmas, to a poet, is that it brings a captive audience. Friends may jib at reading poems, full-length intimidating poems, but a Christmas card can slip under anyone's guard.

The disadvantage of Christmas is that the captive audience includes the widest possible age-range, from toddlers who are just learning to read to great-grandparents who are likely to ring up and ask precisely what line three means. The words should be accessible to all ages, because that's what we feel is needed for a universal message. But it's unnervingly easy to be too simple and sentimental, or too hard and intellectual.

The other problem is that we've been doing this for twenty-eight years, and trying not to repeat oneself becomes progressively more difficult. The cast, after all, is limited: Virgin, carpenter, baby, angels, wise men, and so on. It has for some reason seemed important not to repeat them too much, so absentees have been roped in: the sheepdog left behind to look after the sheep while the shepherds were on duty at the manger; the cat who ought to have been there, even if the evangelists failed to notice it; the robin who is somehow, uncanonically, embedded in Christmas.

We started in 1972, with an old-fashioned second-hand Banda machine, not knowing that this would be the beginning of a tradition which, like all traditions, eventually got the upper hand. The original card consisted of a quotation and a sketch of an oil-lamp, and was done in a café in Wester Ross. After that, writing poetry became serious, and we bought a small Adana press, not realising that we were signing on at the end of a tremendous history; not realising, also, how difficult printing is. We had visions of issuing elegant pamphlets, living a gracious life with a hint of Arts and Crafts about it.

But every year, about August, the deadline looms; and every year the card gets written at the very last minute, in early December, allowing the printer just enough time to get the job done, not always before the overseas postage deadline. The real solution would be to write next year's poem on Boxing Day, while the world is still soaked in the feeling of Christmas. But somehow that never happens.

7

There are technical problems, as well. From quite early days, we used a 6 × 4 card, coloured or white, depending on what was available, cut up at home on the kitchen table. With our first case of type, in the early days, we'd find we'd run out of certain letters, or hyphens or full stops: the poet had to re-write the poem quickly. Then we bought an impressive range of founts, mostly sold off half-price by a typefounder whose store-room, on the banks of the River Coquet in Northumberland, had been flooded: the type was undamaged, though the cardboard boxes and labels had suffered. As the poet grew more accomplished and the subjects more adventurous, we had to adjust the fount and the size of type to fit the card. Long lines weren't appreciated by the printer, nor, indeed, were too many lines of any length. Fancy headings had to give way so that extra verses could be included. And there was always the temptation to illustrate: a drawing (that would fit round the text), a block to be ordered from the block-maker, and then the idiosyncracies of the printing process itself – two printings, one for the drawing, one for the text, hoping they'd settle themselves down comfortably together on their 6 × 4 card. Eventually we settled on a type-face we both liked (Poliphilus, 12 point), which had a distinguished history behind it, looked good, and didn't take up too much room on the card.

So here the poems are, in a new guise. We hope they may be useful, in the way of small, unpretending domestic things.

U. A. Fanthorpe and R. V. Bailey

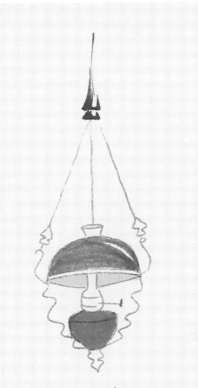

Make we mery bothe more and lasse,
For now is the time of Cristémas!

Christmas 1973

Facsimile of the original card, with drawing and
calligraphy by Rosie Bailey

CENSUS SUMMONS

Census summons
Home to Bethlehem
Royal David's line.
Inns impossible,
Strawy stable
Transforms to
Maternity manger.
Animals attend
Star celebrates

CHRISTMAS

royal David's line

The Sun Capers

The sun capers
Down the goat's short sky.

Nothing fruits but
Holly, flowers but ivy.

Ephemeral
Tinsel, glass balls, whisky,

Crackers, signal
The birth of the god.

MERRY CHRISTMAS!

ANGELS' SONG

Intimates of heaven,
This is strange to us,
The unangelic muddle,
The birth, the human fuss.

We sing a harder carol now:
Holy the donkey in the hay;
Holy the manger made of wood,
Holy the nails, the blood, the clay.

REINDEER REPORT

Chimneys: colder.
Flightpaths: busier.
Driver: Christmas (F)
Still baffled by postcodes.

Children: more
And stay up later.
Presents: heavier.
Pay: frozen.

Mission in spite
Of all this
Accomplished –

MERRY CHRISTMAS!

WHAT THE DONKEY SAW

No room in the inn, of course,
And not that much in the stable,
What with the shepherds, Magi, Mary,
Joseph, the heavenly host –
Not to mention the baby
Using our manger as a cot.
You couldn't have squeezed another cherub in
For love nor money.

Still, in spite of the overcrowding,
I did my best to make them feel wanted.
I could see the baby and I
Would be going places together.

I AM JOSEPH

I am Joseph, carpenter,
Of David's kingly line,
I wanted an heir; discovered
My wife's son wasn't mine.

I am an obstinate lover,
Loved Mary for better or worse.
Wouldn't stop loving when I found
Someone Else came first.

Mine was the likeness I hoped for
When the first-born man-child came.
But nothing of him was me. I couldn't
Even choose his name.

I am Joseph, who wanted
To teach my own boy how to live.
My lesson for my foster son:
Endure. Love. Give.

BC–AD

This was the moment when Before
Turned into After, and the future's
Uninvented timekeepers presented arms.

This was the moment when nothing
Happened. Only dull peace
Sprawled boringly over the earth.

This was the moment when even energetic Romans
Could find nothing better to do
Than counting heads in remote provinces.

And this was the moment
When a few farm workers and three
Members of an obscure Persian sect

Walked haphazard by starlight straight
Into the kingdom of heaven.

Robin's Round

I am the proper
Bird for this season —
Not blessed St Turkey,
Born to be eaten.

I'm man's inedible
Permanent bird.
I dine in his garden,
My spoon is his spade.

I'm the true token
Of Christ the Child-King:
I nest in man's stable,
I eat at man's table,
Through all his dark winters
I sing.

NATIVITIES

Godlings are born racily,

Are excavated
Into life by the strong licks
Of the world-cow, are suckled
By goats, mares, wolves.

Blossom of oak, blossom of broom,
Blossom of meadowsweet
Go to their making.

They erupt through the paternal
Skull fully armed, hatch from an egg,
Or appear, foam-born, in Cyprus, on a shell,
Wearing a great deal of hair and not much else.

This one arrived at the time of the early lambs
Through the usual channels.

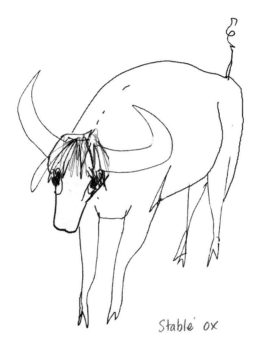

Stable' ox

LULLABY: SANCTUS DEUS

(For Jessica Weeks)

The Angels

Sanctus deus, sleep.
Careful angels keep
Watch from sky's vast sweep.
Nothing moves but sheep.
Lord of heaven, sanctus deus,
Now's the time for sleep.

Mary and Joseph

Baby Jesus, dream
Of some happy theme.
Toothless darling, beam;
Here's no cause to scream.
Mary, Joseph, novice parents,
Whisper: *Baby, dream.*

The Ox

Little man-calf, grow.
You have far to go.
I, the patient, slow,
Stable ox, say so.
Lord of heaven, little man-calf,
My advice is: *Grow.*

Set to music by Nigel Dodd
(see frontispiece)

The Wise Man and the Star

The proper place for stars is in the sky,
Lighting the whole world, but negotiating only
With the highly qualified – master mariners, astro-physicists,
Professionals like ourselves.

This one came unscheduled, nudged us roughly
Out of routine, led us a wild-goose chase,
And perching here, above unspeakable rafters,
Common as a starling on a washing-line,
Whistles to every callow Dick and Harry,
Idling amazed around: 'OK pals, I've done my bit.
Over to you now, Earth.'

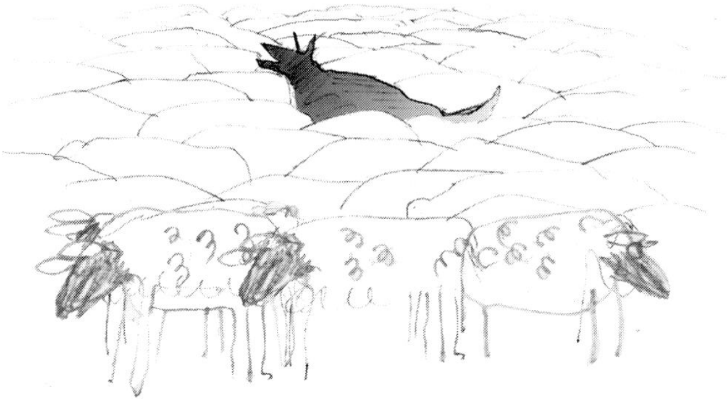

The Sheepdog

After the very bright light,
And the talking bird,
And the singing,
And the sky filled up wi' wings,
And then the silence,

Our lads sez
'We'd better go, then.
Stay, Shep. Good dog, stay.'
So I stayed wi' t' sheep.

After they cum back,
It sounded grand, what they'd seen:
Camels, and kings, and such,
Wi' presents – human sort,
Not the kind you eat –
And a baby. Presents wes for him.
Our lads took him a lamb.

I had to stay behind wi' sheep.
Pity they didn't tek me along, too.
I'm good wi' sheep,
And the baby might have liked a dog
After all that myrrh and such.

The Tree

In the wood I am one of many.
I am felled, sold, chosen
To be sole tree of a house.
I am throned in a gold bucket.
Light is sewn through my branches,
Precious gifts wrapped in silver
Depend from my twigs. Star-crowned,
I am adored by children, cordially hated
By hoovering housewives, distrusted
By Health & Safety Officers, who name me
Fire Hazard. I reign for twelve days,
Then am sacrificed among rubbish,
Where I wither, age, decay.

But every year I rise again indoors,
Hazardous fire of love.

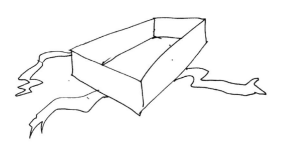

DEAR TRUE LOVE

Leaping and dancing
Means to-ing and fro-ing;
Drummers and pipers –
Loud banging and blowing;
Even a pear-tree
Needs space to grow in.

Goose eggs and gold top
When I'm trying to slim?
And seven swans swimming?
Just where could they swim?

Mine is a small house,
Your gifts are grand;
One ring at a time
Is enough for this hand.

Hens, colly birds, doves –
A gastronome's treat.
But love, I did tell you,
I've given up meat.

Your fairy-tale presents
Are wasted on me.
Just send me your love
And set all the birds free.

Now

After the frantic shopping
The anxious road
After the office parties
The crowded inn

Before the quarterly bills
The stones gathered
Before the January sales
And Stephen, broken

After the carols and lessons
The psalms, the prophets
After the gifts are wrapped
The swaddling clothes

Before the Queen's Speech
A baby's cry
Across the morning suburbs
The Light of the World

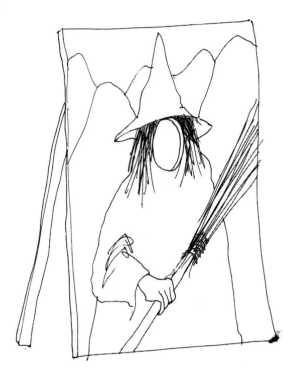

My gift for the child:

No wife, kids, home;
No money sense. Unemployable.
Friends, yes. But the wrong sort —
The workshy, women, wogs,
Petty infringers of the law, persons
With notifiable diseases,
Poll tax collectors, tarts;
The bottom rung.
                          His end?
I think we'll make it
Public, prolonged, painful.

Right, said the baby. *That was roughly
What we had in mind.*

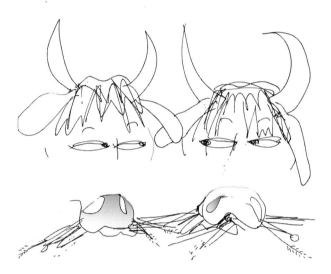

CHRISTMAS SOUNDS

Boeings wing softly over Earth
Humming like enormous *Messiahs*
Bringing everyone home for Christmas;

Children wailing impossible wants,
Housewives worrying in case enough isn't,
Parsons, with prevenient care, sucking Strepsils,

Telly jingling twinkling mistletoe-ing,
Cash tills recording glad tidings of profit,
Office parties munching through menus –

Crackers! Champagne corks!

At the heart of it all, in the hay,
No sound at all but the cattle
Endlessly chewing it over.

CAT IN THE MANGER

In the story, I'm not there.
Ox and ass, arranged at prayer:
But me? Nowhere.

Anti-cat evangelists
How on earth could you have missed
Such an obvious and able
Occupant of any stable?

Who excluded mouse and rat?
The harmless necessary cat.
Who snuggled in with the holy pair?
Me. And my purr.

Matthew, Mark, and Luke and John,
(Who got it wrong,
Who left out the cat)
Remember that,
Wherever He went in this great affair
I was there.

Open House

Queen Ivy and King Holly
Wait at the door to enter
Lord of dark hills, the fir tree
Reigns in the Garden Centre
And the changeling Mistletoe
        Come into the house
        Whoever you are.

Dangerous padded parcels
A red man's chancy load,
With riddled cores of crackers
Watch for their hour to explode
And the changeling Mistletoe
        Come into the house
        Whoever you are.

Black heart of the pudding,
Stuffed heart of the bird,
Green hearts of the brussels sprouts
Signal the holy word
Of ancestral Mistletoe
        Come into this house
        Whoever you are.

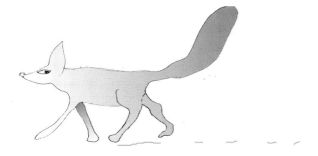

The Invitation

The foxes have holes . . .
Matt. 8:20

The Gloucestershire foxes' message
To the child beyond our sea:
We d' hear thee was born in a stable.
Us dreams uneasy of thee.

Us knows the pack be after thee
Us knows how that du end,
The chase, the kill, the cheering,
Dying wi'out a friend.

So, lover, us makes this suggestion
To thee and thy fam'ly tu:
Come live wi we under Westridge
Where the huntin folk be few.

Thee'll play wi cubs in the sunshine,
Sleep in our snuggest den,
And feed on – well, us'll see to that –
Forget they beastly men.

Maybe thee thinks tis too far off,
Our language strange to thee,
But remember us foxes of Westridge
When thou tires of humanity.

THE CONTRIBUTORS

Not your fault, gentlemen.
We acquit you of the calculatedly
Equivalent gift, the tinsel token.
Mary, maybe, fancied something more practical:
A layette, or at least a premium bond.
Firmly you gave the extravagantly
Useless, your present the unwrapped
Hard-edged stigma of vocation.

Not your fault, beasts,
Who donated your helpless animal
Rectitude to the occasion.
Not yours the message of the goblin
Robin, the red-nosed reindeer,
Nor had you in mind the yearly
Massacre of the poultry innocent,
Whom we judge correct for the feast.

Not your fault, Virgin,
Muddling along in the manger,
With your confused old man,
Your bastard baby, in conditions
No social worker could possibly approve.
How could your improvised, improvident
Holiness predict our unholy family Xmas,
Our lonely overdoses, deepfrozen bonhomie?

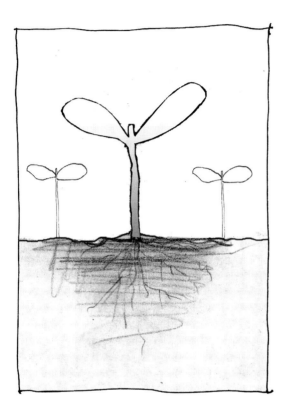

THE GARDENER AT CHRISTMAS

He has done all that needs to be done.
Rake, fork, spade, cleaned and oiled,
Idle indoors; seeds, knotty with destiny, rattle
Inside their paper jackets. The travelling birds

Have left; predictable locals
Mooch in the early dusk.

He dreams of a future in apples,
Of three white lilies in flower,
Of a tree that could bear a man.

He sits back and waits
For it all to happen.

BIRD PSALM

The Swallow said,
He comes like me,
Longed for; unexpectedly.

The superficial eye
Will pass him by,
Said the Wren.

The best singer ever heard.
No one will take much notice,
Said the Blackbird.

The Owl said,
He is who, who is he
Who enters the heart as soft
As my soundless wings, as me.

CHRISTMAS IN ENVELOPES

Monks are at it again, quaffing, carousing;
And stage-coaches, cantering straight out of Merrie England,
In a flurry of whips and fetlocks, sacks and Santas.

Raphael has been roped in, and Botticelli;
Experts predict a vintage year for Virgins.

From the theologically challenged, Richmond Bridge,
Giverny, a lugger by moonlight, doves.   Ours

Costs less than these in money, more in time;
Like them, is hopelessly irrelevant,
But brings, like them, the essential message

love

CHRISTMAS TRAFFIC

'Three, two, one, zero. Lift off'
Signals Mission Control. And off they go
To the dark parts of the planets
In their pressurised spacesuits,
Cocooned in technology, the astronauts.

Mission Control whispers in someone's ear.
'Yes' she says, 'I will.' And in due time
A different traveller makes a quieter journey,
Arriving hungry, naked, true to instructions,
Docking on Earth, taking the one small step.

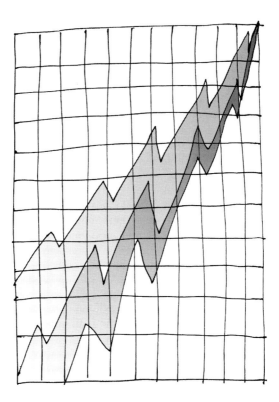

Not the Millennium

Wise men are busy being computer-literate.

There should be a law against confusing
Religion with mathematics.
There was a baby. Born where?
And when? The sources mention
Massacres, prophecies, stars;
They tell a good story, but they don't agree.

So we celebrate at the wrong midnight.
Does it matter? Only dull science expects
An accurate audit. The economy of heaven
Looks for fiestas and fireworks every day,
Every day.
        Be realistic, says heaven:
Expect a miracle.

The Biographers

The genealogist is meticulous.
He harries his subject back to Adam
(Forty-two generations – if you can believe that).

Scene one: the playwright's way in,
Smack in the middle of a river.
Enter a man wearing camel's hair,
Chewing insects.

The novelist deploys more characters
Than Cecil B de Mille: shepherds, angels,
Emperors, wizards, mother (a mute).
He keeps the hero up his sleeve for later.

Babies, bit players, aren't part
Of the mystic's agenda. He starts with aplomb
And a metaphor.

The subject himself: a man not much given
To writing things down. Once
He scraped a message on the ground with a finger.
No one seems to have noticed.
If they did, it was soon scuffed out.

AGNUS DEI: 2001

When the days grow longer, they come,
White as newness. Life and soul
Of the flock, unlike their dingy elders.

In a good year, grow stockier,
Turn into sheep. In a bad year
Leave the world in summer, behind screens,

Smoke, silence, smell of disinfectant.

This one comes with the very early lambs
Always. Doing the things lambs do,
Lord of the dance in the meadow.

He knows where he's going.